BE A REPTILE EXPERT

Be A Pet Expert

By Gemma Barder

Crabtree Publishing
crabtreebooks.com

BE A REPTILE EXPERT

There are many different kinds of reptiles. Some have legs, some slither, some can breathe underwater, some can climb, some can run really fast, and others like to take it slowly. But they all can make amazing pets! If you're thinking of getting a pet reptile or just want to know more about these incredible creatures, you've come to the right place! Learn what type of reptile would suit you best, how to keep your pet happy and healthy, and the fascinating history of these animals.

Crabtree Publishing

crabtreebooks.com   800-387-7650

Published in 2021 by CRABTREE PUBLISHING COMPANY.

First published in 2019 by Wayland
Copyright © Hodder and Stoughton, 2019

Published in Canada
Crabtree Publishing
616 Welland Avenue
St. Catharines, Ontario
L2M 5V6

Published in the United States
Crabtree Publishing
347 Fifth Avenue
Suite 1402-145
New York, NY 10016

Author: Gemma Barder
Editorial director: Kathy Middleton
Editors: Dynamo Limited, Robin Johnson
Cover and interior design: Dynamo Limited
Proofreader: Melissa Boyce
Production coordinator & prepress technician: Samara
Parent Print coordinator: Katherine Kantor

Printed in Canada/042024/CPC20240415

Library and Archives Canada Cataloguing in Publication
Title: Be a reptile expert / by Gemma Barder.
Other titles: Reptiles
Names: Barder, Gemma, author.
Description: Series statement: Be a pet expert |
    Previously published under title: Reptiles. | Includes index.
Identifiers: Canadiana (print) 20200222465 |
    Canadiana (ebook) 2020022249X |
    ISBN 9780778780205 (hardcover) |
    ISBN 9780778780489 (softcover) |
    ISBN 9781427125620 (HTML)
Subjects: LCSH: Reptiles as pets—Juvenile literature. |
    LCSH: Reptiles—Juvenile literature.
Classification: LCC SF459.R4 B37 2021 | DDC j639.3/9—dc23

Photographs:
(l - left, br - bottom right, c - center, tr - top right)
Eric Isselee/Shutterstock: front cover and title page r, 8l; John Cancalosi/Alamy: 6c; Photohobbiest/Shutterstock: 12br; Jessica Girvan1/Shutterstock: 13tr; DWI YULIANTO/Shutterstock: 13br; © Disney Film Company. From "The Jungle Book" directed by Wolfgang Reitherman, 18th October 1967. A.F.Archive/Alamy: 20tl; © Walt Disney Pictures From "Tangled" Entertainment Pictures/Alamy: 20b; Fotos593/Shutterstock: 21t; © 1990 Virgin/Golden Harvest Film. "Teenage Mutant Ninja Turtles" Pictorial Press/Alamy: 21c; fivespots/Shutterstock: 22c, 28br; reptiles4all/Shutterstock: 23c.

Hardcover   978-0-7787-8020-5
Paperback   978-0-7787-8048-9
Ebook (pdf)   978-1-4271-2562-0

Library of Congress Cataloging-in-Publication Data
Names: Barder, Gemma, author.
Title: Be a reptile expert / by Gemma Barder.
Description: New York : Crabtree Publishing Company, 2021. |
    Series: Be a pet expert | Includes index.
Identifiers: LCCN 2020015988 (print) | LCCN 2020015989 (ebook) |
    ISBN 9780778780205 (hardcover) |
    ISBN 9780778780489 (paperback) |
    ISBN 9781427125620 (ebook)
Subjects: LCSH: Reptiles as pets--Juvenile literature.
Classification: LCC SF459.R4 B365 2021 (print) | LCC SF459.R4 (ebook) | DDC 639.3/9--dc23
LC record available at https://lccn.loc.gov/2020015988
LC ebook record available at https://lccn.loc.gov/2020015989

CONTENTS

REMARKABLE
REPTILES

UNDERSTANDING
REPTILES

WORLD OF REPTILES

Reptiles make fun, interesting, and unique pets, and there are plenty of types to choose from. Corn snakes, leopard geckos, Russian tortoises, and bearded dragons are some of the most popular reptile pets.

BEARDED DRAGON

Bearded dragons are not really dragons—and they don't have beards! They are lizards that are active and often enjoy being handled. They like to get out of their tanks at least once a day to climb and run around. They live for up to 10 years and feed on insects and some vegetables.

LEOPARD GECKO

These spotted lizards are friendly and relatively easy to look after. They typically grow up to 10 inches (25 cm) in length, and they feed on live insects.

CORN SNAKE

Corn snakes are calm, gentle, nonvenomous snakes that make great pets. They don't mind being handled for a few minutes, as long as they are used to you! Corn snakes can live for up to 15 years.

RUSSIAN TORTOISE

Russian tortoises are small and more active than their bigger tortoise relatives. They can be kept indoors or outdoors, but most Russian tortoises need to **hibernate** during the winter. These little tortoises are big eaters, so make sure you know which types of plants they prefer.

DID YOU KNOW?

Some reptiles hibernate in cold weather, which means they take a long, deep sleep. Research how to properly care for your reptile during this time.

REMARKABLE REPTILES

Some of the world's most interesting reptiles are facing the threat of **extinction**. From long-lived turtles to a rattlesnake that doesn't rattle, here are just a few of these rare creatures.

ANTIGUAN RACER

This small, gray-brown snake from the Antigua and Barbuda islands in the West Indies is completely harmless to humans and very rare. Scientists have increased the number of these snakes from 50 to more than 1,000 in the past few years and have released some of the snakes raised in **captivity** back into the wild.

GREEN SEA TURTLE

Green sea turtles are shades of green, yellow, black, and brown, with teardrop-shaped shells. These **herbivores** can live for up to 80 years. They can stay under water for up to five hours before they need to come to the surface for air. The coastlines of Australia and Costa Rica are the best places to spot these turtles in the wild.

CUBAN CROCODILE

Scientists believe that the Cuban crocodile is one of the most intelligent and dangerous species of crocodile. This rare reptile can be found only in two areas of Cuba—the Zapata Swamp and the Isle of Youth. Hunting by humans has put this clever crocodile on the list of **critically endangered** animals.

SANTA CATALINA ISLAND RATTLESNAKE

Unlike other rattlesnakes, the Santa Catalina Island rattlesnake doesn't have a working rattle on the end of its body. This unusual snake can be found only on Isla Santa Catalina off the coast of Mexico.

4,675 species — 365 species

There are about 4,675 species of lizards in the world and about 365 species of turtles.

DID YOU KNOW?

The Santa Catalina Island rattlesnake is very good at climbing, which is a skill not found in its rattlesnake cousins.

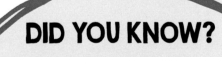

UNDERSTANDING REPTILES

Reptile **instincts** have evolved over thousands of years. Learning about these natural behaviors will help you keep your pet happy.

HISSING

Most snakes are small and harmless. Although many people are afraid of snakes, it actually makes more sense for snakes to be afraid of humans and other large animals. To make itself seem scarier, a snake pushes air through an organ in its throat called the glottis, which makes the snake's famous hissing sound.

HIDING

Turtles are slow-moving creatures, so if they feel threatened they can't just run for cover under the nearest bush. Instead, a turtle pulls its legs and head inside its tough shell to keep its soft parts protected. If your turtle does this when you approach, it could be feeling scared or anxious.

TAIL WHIPPING

A lizard's tail is one of its most powerful body parts. If your usually tame pet tries to whip you with its tail, you should leave it alone. Lizards use their tails against **predators**, so if your pet is feeling threatened give it time to calm down before handling it again.

TONGUE FLICKING

You will often see reptiles such as snakes and lizards flicking their tongues in and out. This is a way for them to check out their environments. With each flick, reptiles collect **particles** from the air that help them sniff out food or alert them that a predator is nearby.

HATCHLINGS

Reptile babies are some of the toughest little creatures on the planet. They start to look after themselves at a very early age and have amazing instincts.

TURTLES AND TORTOISES

Turtles and tortoises lay two to 12 eggs at a time. Before laying the eggs, females create nests on land by digging away at soil or sand. When a baby is ready to hatch, it uses an egg tooth on the end of its nose to break the shell and nudge its way out. The tooth falls off as the **hatchling** grows up.

DID YOU KNOW?

Tortoises live on land, while turtles live in water some or nearly all of the time.

SNAKES

Some snakes give birth to live babies, but most snakes lay eggs. A snake's egg is soft and leathery, not hard like a chicken's egg. Snakes can produce between one and 100 hatchlings at a time. Although some pythons will guard their eggs until they hatch, most baby snakes are left to take care of themselves!

LIZARDS

Like snakes, lizards can either give birth to live young or lay eggs, depending on the species. One thing all baby lizards have in common is their ability to survive. They take care of themselves, eating the same food and protecting themselves from predators like adult lizards do.

65 days

100 days

Turtle eggs take an average of 65 days to hatch, while tortoise eggs can take up to 100 days.

HOME SWEET HOME

Reptiles need very special homes to mimic their habitats in the wild. Discover what you need to keep your reptile healthy and happy.

TORTOISES

The type of house a tortoise needs depends on its breed and age. Younger tortoises may need heat lamps or heating pads to regulate their body temperatures. Older tortoises are happy to live outdoors, as long as it's not too cold. Temperatures below 59 °Fahrenheit (15 °C) can be dangerous for tortoises.

A tortoise home needs a large area for the tortoise to wander around in. Tortoises love to climb, so add in a few large rocks for your pet to explore. Finally, all tortoises like quiet places to sleep, so make sure your tortoise's home has a covered area.

SNAKES

Snakes come in all shapes and sizes, but they all need to live in vivariums. A vivarium is a glass tank that allows you to control the temperature and keep an eye on your pet. A general rule is that the tank should be at least two-thirds the length of your fully grown snake.

Snakes like to hide, explore, or just wrap their bodies around things. The bottom of the tank should be lined with soil or sand, then filled with branches, rocks, and plants for your pet to explore. Ask for advice from a pet store to make sure you include the right types of plants for your breed of snake.

TURTLES

Turtles live on land and in water, so your pet's tank will need to have both of these elements in it. You can use a special turtle tank, or a large fish tank would also work well. Turtles love light and heat to **bask** in, so you will need to add a lamp to the top of your tank. These reptiles need UVA and UVB light (two types of **UV light**), so make sure the lamp can take both types of bulbs.

The tank will need to be heated to around 81 °Fahrenheit (27 °C) to keep your turtle cozy. Most importantly, you will need to create a home where your turtle can get in and out of the water. Use smooth rocks and logs to create an easy path for your pet.

LIZARDS

A lizard needs a warm tank or vivarium to live in. The size of your pet's tank will depend on the size and type of lizard, but all lizards need UV light and some **humidity**. Getting the level of humidity wrong can cause your pet to get sick.

Your lizard will be happiest in a tank with some shallow water and plenty of places to climb and hide. However, there are many different types of lizards, so do your research to make sure your lizard has the healthiest and happiest home.

DID YOU KNOW?

Geckos are the only lizards that have vocal cords. Every other lizard communicates using body language.

LOVE AND ATTENTION

Reptiles need a lot of care, so do your research before bringing your pet home. Make sure you are prepared to do whatever your pet needs to be healthy and happy.

SNAKE LOVE

Once you have set up a safe home for your snake, it's time to think about food and cleaning. All snakes are **carnivores**, but what they eat depends on the species. Corn snakes and milk snakes can be fed baby or adult mice, depending on the snake's size. Most snake food can be frozen and then thawed when it is feeding time.

How often you clean your snake's home will depend on the size of your pet. Snakes don't poop and pee as often as other animals, but you should clean any **soiled** areas right away. Change your snake's water each day and keep an eye out for any mold building up on the sides of the tank.

DID YOU KNOW?

A snake's food should be no bigger than the widest part of its body.

TORTOISE CARE

Tortoises LOVE vegetables. Salad and other vegetables should make up 80 percent of your pet's diet, with a little fruit added as a treat. Add powdered calcium and vitamin D3 to your tortoise's food once or twice a week to help keep its shell strong. Change your tortoise's water and remove any droppings or wet bedding each day. Clean your tortoise's home thoroughly and change all the bedding every two to three weeks.

FACT FILE

DINNERTIME!

How often will you need to feed your reptile?

Corn snake: once a week

Milk snake: every 10–14 days

Leopard gecko: every other day

Bearded dragon: once a day

Tortoise: five times a week

Turtle: every two to three days

LOOKING AFTER LIZARDS

It is important to know as much as you can about your species of lizard before you bring it home. Some lizards, such as bearded dragons, don't mind being handled, but others find it stressful. Leopard geckos will eat only live **prey** such as crickets and cockroaches, so If you don't want to keep creepy-crawlies in your house you might want to choose another pet!

REPTILE RULES

Here are some tips on the dos and don'ts of looking after your reptile.

DO:

Research your reptile! Find out everything you need to know about your pet before you bring it home. ✔

Use a heat lamp. Most reptiles need some form of heat, so make sure you know the correct temperature and the length of time your pet likes to bask. ✔

Wash your hands before and after handling your pet because some reptiles carry a bacteria called salmonella. ✔

Consider adopting an older reptile because some can live for a VERY long time. ✔

Handle turtles with care. A cracked turtle shell can lead to infection. ✔

Find out how big your reptile will grow and make sure you have a big enough vivarium or tank. ✔

DON'T:

Don't use water straight from the tap for your reptile to drink or to swim in. Use either dechlorinated or fresh spring water. ✗

Don't use wood chips, especially in turtle tanks, because they can be deadly if swallowed. ✗

Don't leave a tortoise outside in the cold. If your tortoise usually lives outdoors, bring it into your home on cold days. ✗

Don't put different reptile species in the same tank. Each reptile needs to be cared for in different ways. ✗

Don't handle your reptile too soon after it has eaten because that could be harmful to its digestion. ✗

Don't give your pet too much food. Overweight reptiles are at greater risk of getting sick. ✗

✔ FOOD FOR REPTILES ✗

Bearded dragons: carrots, cabbage, and crickets

Corn snakes: frozen mice that have been thawed

Leopard geckos: live mealworms and crickets

Milk snakes: frozen mice that have been thawed

Tortoises: leafy greens and soft fruit

Turtles: vegetables and small fish

Bearded dragons: avocado

Corn snakes: crickets

Leopard geckos: fireflies or glowworms

Milk snakes: food bigger than the width of its body

Tortoises and turtles: processed meat and spinach

SLITHER THROUGH TIME

Reptiles have been around for a very long time. Find out how they went from ruling Earth to being a popular pet.

EVOLUTION

Fossils of the first species of lizard date to around 240 million years old. About a million years later, some of these lizards evolved without legs and became snakes.

310–320 MILLION YEARS AGO

240 MILLION YEARS AGO

252–66 MILLION YEARS AGO

THE FIRST REPTILE

The first known reptile is believed to be *Hylonomus*. It was the first **reptilian** creature to live on land and looked very similar to the lizards we see today. It was about 8 inches (20 cm) long and fed on insects and snails.

DINO TIME

This period of time is called the Mesozoic Era or the Age of the Dinosaurs. These reptiles once ruled Earth, but they became extinct about 66 million years ago.

DID YOU KNOW?

Scientists think the chicken might be the closest living relative to *Tyrannosaurus rex*.

ROOM FOR REPTILES

It wasn't until the early twentieth century that reptiles became popular as pets. Before then it was hard to keep homes warm enough for these **cold-blooded** animals to survive.

66 MILLION YEARS AGO	1920s	TODAY

BIRDS EVOLVED FROM DINOSAURS

We can see the **evolution** of dinosaurs in many creatures alive today, such as lizards, snakes, and other reptiles. We can see it in birds too. They have scaly feet and feathers like many dinosaurs had!

POPULAR PETS

Reptiles are more popular than ever! It is estimated there are more than 9 million reptiles kept as pets in the United States.

SCALY STARDOM

From superheroes to the last of its kind, these famous reptiles are known around the world.

BHUTAN 30^{CH}

WALT DISNEY'S THE JUNGLE BOOK

KAA

Kaa is a giant, powerful snake from Rudyard Kipling's *The Jungle Book*, written in 1894. The story focuses on a young boy named Mowgli who is raised by a pack of wolves in the jungle. Kaa is a wise snake who helps Mowgli when he is in danger.

DID YOU KNOW?

In the movie versions of *The Jungle Book*, Kaa's character is changed to Mowgli's enemy.

PASCAL

In 2010, a chameleon named Pascal became one of Disney's best-loved reptiles in the movie *Tangled*. As Rapunzel's best (and only) friend, Pascal encourages her to leave the tower and follow her dreams. He is by her side through all her adventures, changing color as he goes!

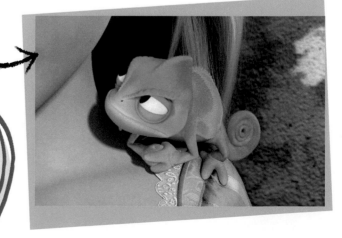

DID YOU KNOW?

Chameleons change color based on their moods, not to blend in to their environments. They have special skin cells that reflect light in different ways.

LONESOME GEORGE

For many years, scientists believed that a species of giant tortoise called the Pinta Island tortoise was extinct. However, in 1971, a scientist who was studying snails on Pinta Island (one of the Galapagos Islands) spotted one of these rare reptiles. A team of scientists later named the tortoise Lonesome George. They hoped that a mate could be found for him, but unfortunately he was the last of his kind. Lonesome George died in 2012 when he was about 100 years old.

TEENAGE MUTANT NINJA TURTLES

In the 1980s, two friends came up with the idea of teenage crime-fighting turtles and created a comic book starring the superheroes. The comic was a hit and soon toys and a cartoon series were made. During the 1990s, *Teenage Mutant Ninja Turtles* was one of the biggest shows on TV. The turtles were given a new look in 2018 and are still popular today.

FACT FILE

How well do you know the Teenage Mutant Ninja Turtles?

■ They are named after famous Italian artists: Leonardo, Donatello, Michelangelo, and Raphael.

■ Their favorite food is pizza (although real turtles would get really sick if they ate pizza!).

■ They are trained by a rat named Splinter who is a master of ninja moves.

■ They hide in an underground headquarters during the day and come out at night to fight crime.

RECORD-BREAKING REPTILES

3,000 species

600 venomous

There are more than 3,000 species of snakes in the world, and only 600 of them are **venomous**.

Reptiles come in all shapes and sizes. Take a look at the snakes, lizards, and tortoises that have become record-breakers!

Pythons can grow to extreme lengths in the wild.

LONGEST SNAKE

A reticulated python named Medusa holds the world record for the longest snake in captivity. Medusa is 25.2 feet (7.67 m) long and spends her time as an attraction in a haunted house show in Kansas City, Missouri.

LONGEST FANGS

Inside its flat head, the extremely venomous Gaboon viper hides the world's longest snake fangs, which can measure up to 1.6 inches (4 cm) long. Unsurprisingly, this deadly viper releases the most venom of any snake.

 Open wide!

FINISH

Do you think it won the race?

FASTEST TORTOISE

Tortoises are not known for their speed, but a pet tortoise (like the one shown above) named Bertie is officially the fastest tortoise in the world. The speedy reptile from the United Kingdom can go as fast as 0.6 miles per hour (0.9 kph).

LAZIEST TURTLE

According to Guinness World Records, the laziest turtle is the Cantor's giant softshell turtle. It moves from its favorite spot on the riverbed only when it needs to breathe air—which is about twice a day. The rest of the time it lies and waits for prey to come to it!

BIGGEST LIZARD

The Komodo dragon is by far the largest lizard in the world, so it is not kept as a pet. It can grow up to 10 feet (3 m) long and weighs up to 300 pounds (136 kg). Its venomous bite can take down large prey with a single snap. This large lizard can run up to 12 miles per hour (20 kph).

THE REPTILE FILES

Do you think you know everything about reptiles? Think again, because these incredible creatures are about to get even more interesting!

1 REPTILES ARE (ALMOST) EVERYWHERE

Reptiles can be found on every continent except Antarctica, where it is far too cold for them to survive.

2 SNAKES AREN'T SCARY

Only about 7 percent of all snake species are harmful to humans—except in Australia, where there are more species of venomous snakes than nonvenomous snakes!

3 THEY ARE COVERED IN KERATIN

All snakes and many lizards are covered in scales made of a substance called keratin. That is the same substance that human fingernails are made of.

4 SEA TURTLES ARE REALLY OLD

Sea turtles have been on the planet for 220 million years! On average, a sea turtle lives to be around 80 years old.

5 REPTILES AREN'T THE SMARTEST CREATURES

Although their ancient ancestors ruled Earth, reptiles aren't as smart as other pets. A reptile's brain is about one-tenth the size of a cat's brain!

THE RIGHT REPTILE

With so many reptiles to choose from, would a gecko, snake, or tortoise be right for you?

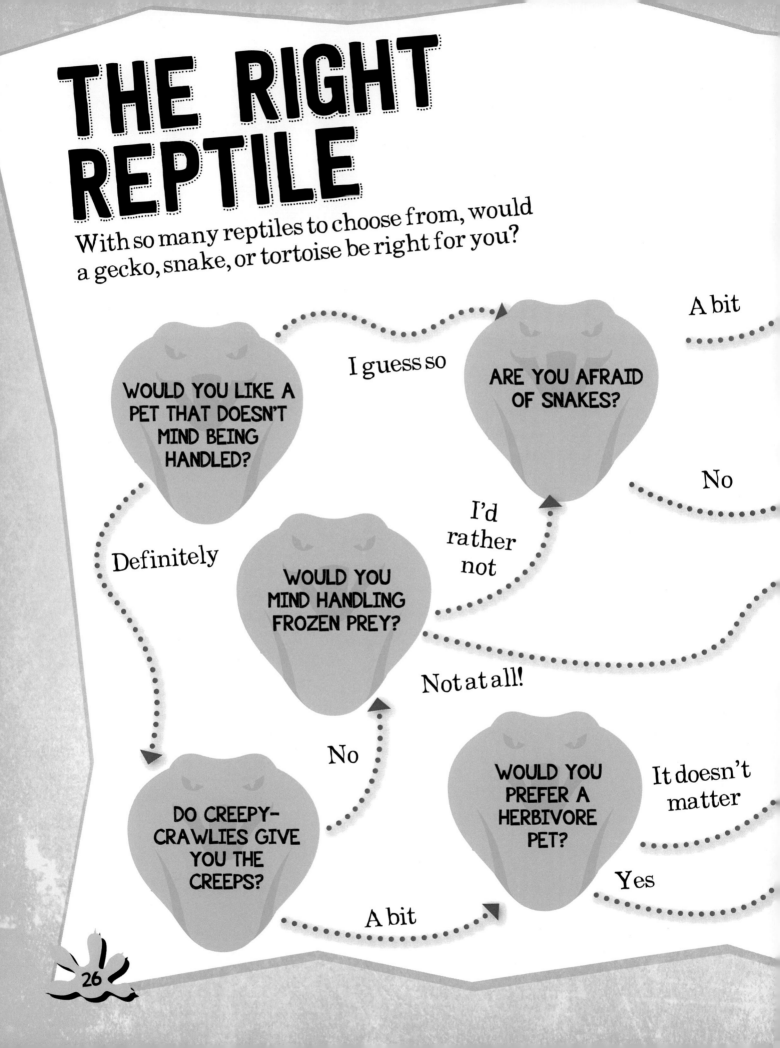

WOULD YOU LIKE A PET THAT DOESN'T MIND BEING HANDLED?

I guess so

A bit

ARE YOU AFRAID OF SNAKES?

No

Definitely

WOULD YOU MIND HANDLING FROZEN PREY?

I'd rather not

Not at all!

No

DO CREEPY-CRAWLIES GIVE YOU THE CREEPS?

WOULD YOU PREFER A HERBIVORE PET?

It doesn't matter

Yes

A bit

WOULD YOU PREFER AN ACTIVE PET?

Yes

I don't care

WHAT'S BETTER: CRAWLING OR SLITHERING?

Crawling

Slithering

WOULD YOU LIKE TO KEEP YOUR PET INDOORS OR OUTDOORS?

Indoors

Outdoors

Not always!

DO YOU LIKE TO TAKE THINGS SLOWLY?

Yes

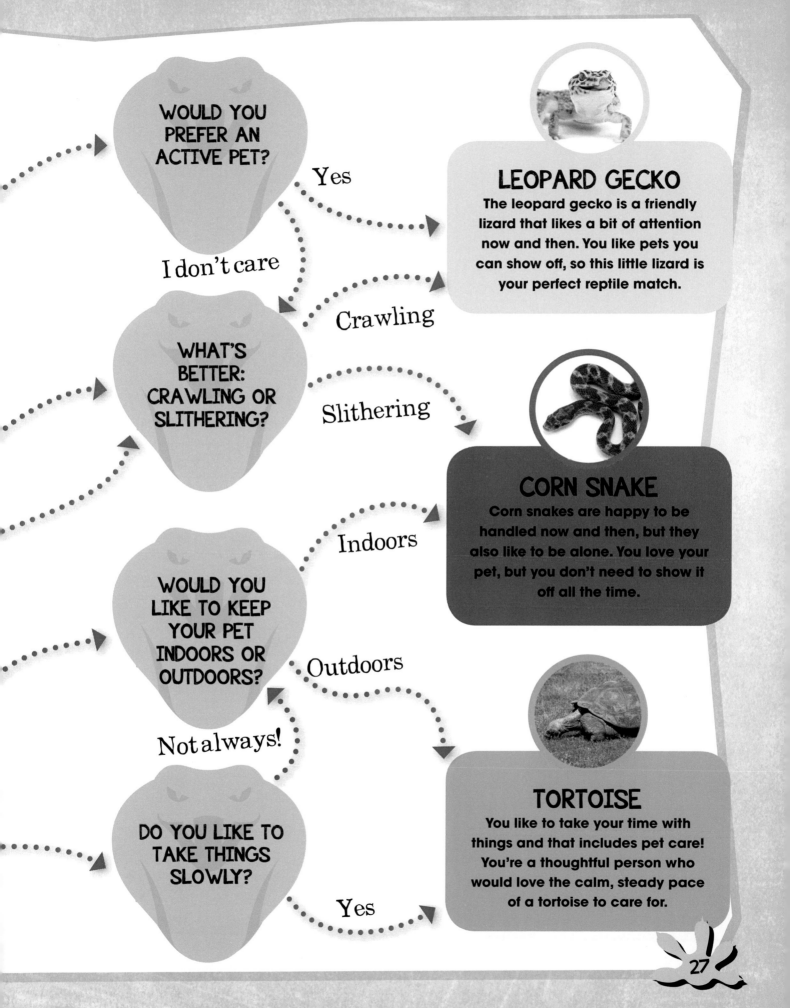

LEOPARD GECKO
The leopard gecko is a friendly lizard that likes a bit of attention now and then. You like pets you can show off, so this little lizard is your perfect reptile match.

CORN SNAKE
Corn snakes are happy to be handled now and then, but they also like to be alone. You love your pet, but you don't need to show it off all the time.

TORTOISE
You like to take your time with things and that includes pet care! You're a thoughtful person who would love the calm, steady pace of a tortoise to care for.

QUIZ!

Now that you've read all about reptiles, do you think you are a pet expert? Take this quiz to find out!

1 WHAT IS A LEOPARD GECKO'S FAVORITE FOOD?

a) raw fish
b) live insects
c) lettuce

2 WHAT IS UNUSUAL ABOUT THE SANTA CATALINA ISLAND RATTLESNAKE?

a) it doesn't have a rattling tail
b) it's not a snake
c) it's a herbivore

3 HOW DO MOST LIZARDS SMELL THINGS?

a) with their ears
b) with their feet
c) by tasting the air with their tongues

4 WHAT DOES A SNAKE EGG FEEL LIKE?

a) soft and leathery
b) hard and smooth
c) like sandpaper

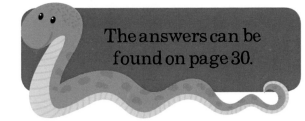

The answers can be found on page 30.

6 WHY SHOULD YOU WASH YOUR HANDS AFTER HANDLING YOUR REPTILE?

a) in case it pooped on you
b) to make your hands smell nice
c) to stop the spread of salmonella

7 WHAT IS THE CLOSEST LIVING ANIMAL TO A *T-REX*?

a) the tortoise
b) the chicken
c) the dog

5 HOW OFTEN SHOULD YOU FEED A CORN SNAKE?

a) once a day
b) once a week
c) once a month

WHAT WAS THE NAME OF RAPUNZEL'S CHAMELEON FRIEND IN THE MOVIE *TANGLED?*

a) Peter
b) Pascal
c) Pasha

WHAT IS SPECIAL ABOUT A GABOON VIPER'S FANGS?

a) they aren't venomous
b) they aren't sharp
c) they are the longest of any snake

WHAT PERCENTAGE OF SNAKES ARE HARMFUL TO HUMANS?

a) 50 percent
b) 22 percent
c) 7 percent

GLOSSARY

adopt
To take care of a pet that once belonged to someone else and needs a new home

bacteria
Very small living things that often cause disease

bask
To lie in a bright, warm place

captivity
An enclosed space removed from the wild

carnivore
An animal that eats mainly meat

cold-blooded
Describing an animal whose body temperature changes with the temperature of its surroundings

critically endangered
Describing animals at high risk of dying out in the wild

dechlorinated
Describing something that has had the chemical chlorine removed from it

digestion
The process by which food is broken down after eating

evolution
The process where living things change from one species to another over millions of years

extinction
When a species of animal or plant has died out

fossil
The remains of a living thing that died long ago, usually preserved in rock

hatchling
A baby animal that has just emerged from an egg

herbivore
An animal that eats mainly plants

hibernate
To enter a state of deep sleep during cold months

humidity
The amount of water in the air

instinct
Natural behavior that is not taught or learned

particle
A tiny piece or amount of something

predator
An animal that hunts and eats other animals

prey
Animals that are hunted and eaten by other animals

reptilian
Of or relating to reptiles

salmonella
A type of bacteria that causes severe food poisoning

soiled
Covered in pee or poop

UV light
Light rays that are invisible to the human eye and can cause sunburn

venomous
Having or producing venom, a poisonous substance made by some animals that is injected into prey, usually by biting or stinging

INDEX